J. WESTON
WALCH
PUBLISHER

BASIC OCCUPATIONAL MATH

SECOND EDITION

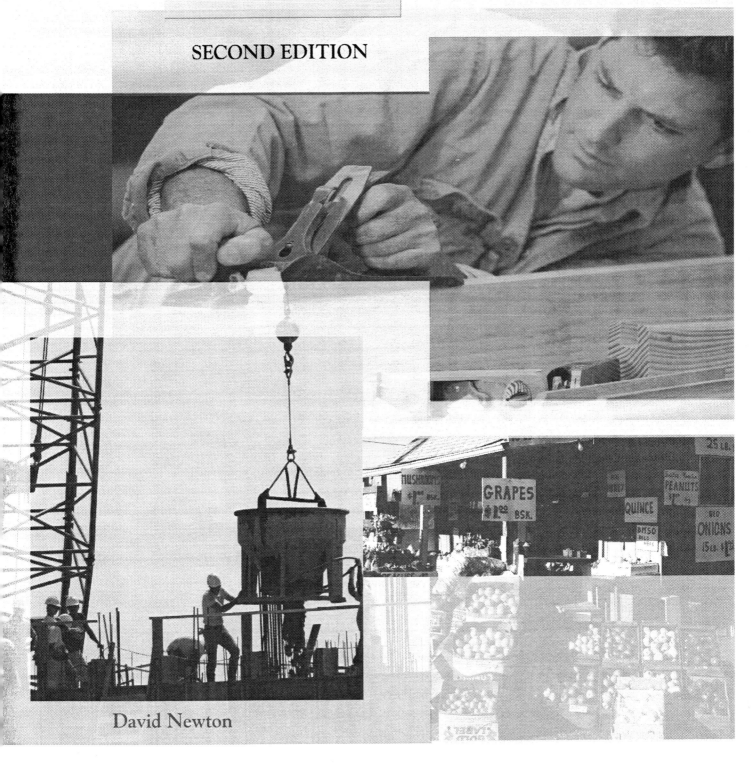

David Newton

User's Guide
to
Walch Reproducible Books

Purchasers of this book are granted the right to reproduce all pages where this symbol appears.

This permission is limited to a single teacher, for classroom use only.

Any questions regarding this policy or requests to purchase further reproduction rights should be addressed to:

Permissions Editor
J. Weston Walch, Publisher
321 Valley Street • P.O. Box 658
Portland, Maine 04104-0658

1   2   3   4   5   6   7   8   9   10

ISBN 0-8251-4355-1

Copyright © 1990, 2002
J. Weston Walch, Publisher
P. O. Box 658 • Portland, Maine 04104-0658
www.walch.com

Printed in the United States of America

CONTENTS

TO THE TEACHER

Basic Occupational Math is an introduction to basic mathematical operations required in a broad range of occupations. Among the jobs mentioned in the book are catering, clerical work, cooking, construction work, auto mechanics, electronic repair, medical and laboratory technical work, stockroom work, clerical work, typesetting, interior decorating, drafting, carpentry, painting, masonry, roofing, truck driving, nursery management, tool-and-die work, dressmaking, and farming.

Basic Occupational Math illustrates mathematical operations performed both manually and with a calculator. Practice problems are arranged in order of difficulty. Not all students are expected to solve all problems.

The teacher's guide provides suggestions for teaching and a complete answer key. A diagnostic pretest and a posttest for each chapter are included in handy reproducible form.

David E. Newton
Ashland, OR
2002

TEACHING SUGGESTIONS

1. Workers in the community can be an important asset in a class on occupational mathematics. Some may be willing to talk to your class about the role of mathematics on the job. Others may be willing to invite students to the job site. Students might interview workers to collect examples of math problems to use in class.

2. The Internet is an invaluable source of information on mathematics in a variety of occupations. Students can type search words into popular search engines to find the information they need.

3. Newspaper articles and advertisements provide a host of math-related topics for discussion in class.

Chapter 1: Whole Numbers

Place Value in Numbers

1. You may want to distinguish between the two related terms *numerals* (or *digits*) and *numbers*. Numerals are the counting numbers from 0 to 9. Numbers, such as 482, consist of numerals whose value depends on their place (location) within the number. Thus, the 4 in 482 has a value of 400 because of its position in the hundreds place in the number.

2. Remind students that the 0 that precedes a decimal point in a decimal number is written for purposes of clarification. The decimal point in 0.162 is less likely to get lost than it might in .162.

3. Students may better understand the meaning of place value by saying numbers aloud and hearing them spoken aloud as they point to each digit in a number.

4. The word *and* is properly used in reading a number only to indicate a decimal point. Thus the number 506 is read "five hundred six," not "five hundred and six."

Adding Whole Numbers

1. To minimize the possibility of error, students should become accustomed to writing numbers neatly, in proper order, and with place values aligned in mathematical operations.

2. When you teach the process of *carrying*, remind students of the place value of numbers. Carrying over a digit to the next higher place must have a logical basis, rather than "something you just have to do" in a calculation.

3. Familiarize yourself with the calculators your students use.

Subtracting Whole Numbers

1. The concept of *borrowing* in subtraction makes sense to students if they understand place value in a number.

2. Unlike addition, where addends can be combined in any sequence, the order in which terms are subtracted is significant. For that reason, terminology (minuend, subtrahend, and difference) is important in subtraction.

3. You may want to teach students to check the answer to a subtraction problem by adding the answer (difference) to the subtrahend in order to get the minuend.

4. Point out to students that Practice Problems 8 through 10 involve more than one step. The answers to these problems may be found by either (1) adding a series of numbers first and then subtracting that sum from a total or (2) subtracting each number from the total, one at a time.

Multiplying Whole Numbers

1. Be sure that students have mastered the basic multiplication tables before they study this section.

2. Some problems require more than one step. Remind students to solve each problem one step at a time.

Dividing Whole Numbers

1. You may prefer to introduce division as repeated subtraction. Thus, the division of 35 by 7 can be thought of as the number of times 7 can be subtracted from 35. The answer is 5 times.

$$35 - 7 = 28 - 7 = 21 - 7 = 14 - 7 = 7 - 7 = 0$$

By teaching division this way, the concept of a *remainder* becomes obvious. Consider, for example, the division problem $25 \div 7$:

$$25 - 7 = 18 - 7 = 11 - 7 = 4$$

That is, 7 can be subtracted from 25 three times, and 4 *remains* after the last subtraction.

2. Understanding the terminology—dividend, divisor, and quotient—can be helpful. Unlike multiplication, where the order of factors is not important, order in division is significant: $25 \div 7 \neq 7 \div 25$.

Chapter 2: Fractions

Fraction Terminology

1. The fundamental rule of fractions is that you can multiply or divide *both* numerator and denominator by the *same* number without changing the value of the fraction. However, adding to or subtracting from the numerator or denominator does change the value of the fraction.

2. Encourage students to reduce fractions to lowest terms to simplify calculations.

Adding Fractions

1. The method for finding a common denominator will not necessarily produce the least common denominator. The method for finding the LCD is beyond the scope of this book.

2. Measurements in the British system are sometimes expressed in decimal form, such as 8.3 inches. They are more commonly expressed as fractions, such as $8\frac{7}{8}$ inches. You can devise many additional practical problems by having students use rulers and yardsticks to measure objects and then perform operations with those measurements.

Subtracting Fractions

1. Some students may solve problems more easily if they draw the conditions given in the problem.

Multiplying Fractions

1. Some students may be able to multiply the numerator and denominator of fractions directly, as

$$\frac{2}{4} \times \frac{1}{5} = \frac{1}{10}$$

Others will find it useful to write the intermediary step.

$$\frac{2}{4} \times \frac{1}{5} = \frac{2}{20} = \frac{1}{10}$$

2. Dividing the numerator and denominator of a fraction by a common factor always makes a problem easier to solve. Some teachers object to calling this process *canceling* because the term has no mathematical meaning. They prefer to emphasize that some common factor has been divided out in both numerator and denominator.

3. Explain to students that any whole number can be thought of as a fraction whose denominator is 1.

4. Practice Problem 5 can also be solved by proportions, although that procedure is not introduced until Chapter 6.

Dividing Fractions

1. The key to dividing fractions is inverting the divisor. Once that step has been taken, a division problem becomes a multiplication problem.

2. Dividing fractions may be difficult for students because it is hard to visualize the process. Students may not be clear about what goes into what. Temporarily replacing the fractions in the problem with whole numbers may clarify what goes into what. Once the divisor and dividend have been sorted out, the original fractions can be restored and the calculation made.

3. A simple sketch may help some students understand how to set up and solve a problem.

Chapter 3: Decimals and Percents

Introduction

1. Remind students that a lone zero precedes a decimal point for clarity only and is not involved in any mathematical operation.

2. Many students find that decimal problems are easier to solve than fraction problems, especially with a calculator.

3. News articles, feature stories, and advertisements contain prices, costs, and percents that can be used to construct additional problems.

Adding Decimals

1. Emphasize aligning addends so that decimal points and digits are in the proper column.

2. You may want to talk about rounding off as an exercise in logic. Without instruction, students should be able to decide how much precision makes sense for any given answer.

Subtracting Decimals

1. Remind students that trailing zeros after a decimal make no difference in a mathematical operation. That is, 45.32 is mathematically equivalent to 45.320 or 45.3200 or 45.32000, and so on.

2. Solutions with negative numbers are not uncommon. Students are familiar with everyday situations involving temperature or money, for example. You might ask what the temperature would be if it fell 10° from 5°C. Or you could ask students what checking account balance they would have if they wrote a check for $25.00 against an account with a previous balance of $15.00.

A lesson on negative numbers can begin with handheld calculators, which report answers quickly without requiring students to perform calculations. After seeing negative answers appear on the calculator, students can then focus on what those numbers mean.

Multiplying Decimals

1. Multiplying decimals differs from multiplying whole numbers only in respect to the placement of decimal points. Concentrate on making sure that students understand how to decide where the decimal point belongs in an answer. Also, it is not necessary to align decimal points when setting up the original problem.

2. Estimating answers is a skill that can be taught and used in any mathematical calculation. You may want to remind students that estimation works with all kinds of problems.

Dividing Decimals

1. Caution students to use care in moving decimal points in division problems.

2. Students may mistakenly believe that a smaller number cannot be divided by a larger number (for example, $4 \div 7$). Make sure they understand that this idea is incorrect.

3. Dividing whole numbers and decimals can produce answers with decimals that extend indefinitely. Discuss with students how to determine the number of decimal places in an answer. A rule of thumb might be that an answer should never be more precise than the least precise number in the problem.

Operations with Fractions and Decimals

1. All fractions are essentially division problems, even odd-looking fractions like those on pages 68–69. Thus, the expression

$$\frac{0.32}{\frac{4}{5}}$$

can be thought of as $0.32 \div \frac{4}{5}$ (or $0.32 \div [4 \div 5]$) and—in this form—easily solved.

It is worthwhile having students memorize at least some of the fraction-decimal equivalents on page 68.

Percents

1. A good source of additional exercises is any sale advertisement. You can ask students to calculate, for example, 40% off $199.95.

Chapter 4: Powers, Roots, and Geometric Figures

Roots and Powers

1. Point out to students the difference between a square root sign (radical) ($\sqrt{}$) and a division sign ($\overline{\rceil}$).

2. You may wish to demonstrate how to use tables of powers and roots featured in many textbooks.

3. Help students learn to calculate roots and powers on their own calculators.

Geometric Figures

1. Students will benefit from making a sketch of most of the problems in this section.

2. The technical name for a six-faced rectangular solid is a parallepiped.

Linear, Angular, and Circular Measurement

1. Students should either memorize the formulas on pages 81–82 or have copies available.

2. As an enrichment exercise, you might ask students to read about the discovery of pi and about efforts to calculate its precise value.

3. Review with students the various mathematical symbols for multiplication. (See page 18).

4. In some occupations, angles must be measured precisely in minutes and seconds. You may wish to discuss in some detail this level of precision in angle measurement.

5. A value of 3.14 for π is usually adequate in problems involving decimals; use $\frac{22}{7}$ in problems with fractions.

Area

1. Students should memorize the formulas on pages 85–86 or have copies available.

2. Solving for linear dimensions where the area of a figure is known is discussed on pages 122–125.

3. Be sure that students understand all possible abbreviations for square units, such as sq in and in^2.

Volume

1. Students should memorize the formulas on page 92 or have copies available.

2. You may want to review with students how to use calculator memory buttons (M+, M–, and M) to solve problems that have more than one step.

Chapter 5: Measuring Systems and Devices

Introduction

1. Measurement is a skill with which most students are familiar. The advantage of that familiarity is that you probably do not have to spend much time on the basics of weighing, finding lengths, and measuring volumes. The disadvantage is that students may be unaware of some fundamental aspects of measurement. For example, measurement is often regarded as the first step in collecting true, accurate, and precise information. It may come as a surprise to students that *all* measurements, inherently and unavoidably, contain some degree of uncertainty or error. Awareness of that error, specifically its magnitude, is crucial in understanding error terms and tolerance in measurement.

2. Discuss with students possible sources of error in measurement and what can be done to reduce its effect.

3. Point out that the symbol ± is read "plus or minus."

4. The only common liquid with a negative (convex) meniscus is mercury. Reading the meniscus on a mercury thermometer requires particular attention and skill.

5. Collect a variety of measuring devices—balances, graduated cylinders and beakers, pipettes and burettes, meter- and yardsticks—for students to examine. You may be able to borrow these devices from your school science laboratory or a local workplace.

6. Invite a representative from the local water or power company to visit your class to describe the meters and measuring devices used at his or her company.

7. Notice that most water meters are calibrated in *cubic feet,* but water charges may be translated into the number of *gallons* used. The conversion factor is 1 cubic foot = 7.48 gallons.

8. Precisely speaking, the kilogram (kg) is a unit of mass, not weight. In everyday life, however, we use the word to mean both an object's mass and the force that gravity exerts on that mass. Earth's gravity pulls on a kilogram of mass with a force of 2.2 pounds.

Measuring Systems

1. You may want to allow some class time for a discussion about the advantages and disadvantages of the British (customary) and metric systems of measurement. Many industries are finding it necessary to convert to metric measurements in order to compete in international markets.

2. The factor-label method for conversions provides a quick and foolproof way of making any conversion of measurement units.

The Metric System

1. You might look for examples of unusual metric prefixes. Students may be familiar with *mega* and *kilo,* for example, but not with *pico* and *nano.*

2. The factor-label method of making conversions may require more than one step. For example, students may use two conversion factors, kg to g and then g to cg, to change 3.5 kg to cg. Students will benefit from additional practice with two- and three-step problems.

Measuring Devices

1. Only metric micrometers are discussed in the text. You may wish to compare them with micrometers graduated in customary units.

2. Ideally, every student should have a chance to hold, examine, and use the measuring devices described in this chapter. A local industrial-technology teacher may be able to lend you some of these instruments.

3. Invite a tradesperson who uses these measuring devices to visit.

Chapter 6: Mathematical Formulas; Ratios and Proportions

Mathematical Formulas

1. Remind students how much they already know about formulas—for example, for finding area and volume. (See Chapter 4.)

2. This chapter presents two methods of solving for an unknown.

   a. Substitute known values into the formula and then solve for the unknown.

   b. First, solve the formula algebraically for the term of interest. Then substitute known numerical values to solve for the unknown. This method is preferred if the formula is to be used over and over again. For example, a bank employee may repeatedly have to calculate the principal (p) on a loan knowing the interest (i) and rate (r) charged on the loan and the time (t) over which it extends. In this case, it may be more efficient to solve first algebraically for principal in the formula $i = prt$ ($p = \frac{i}{rt}$) and then substitute known numerical values in each specific case.

3. Emphasize the importance of treating both sides of an equation in the same way, by adding or subtracting, multiplying or dividing by the same number on each side.

4. Review with students the variety of ways to express multiplication.

$$lwh = l \times w \times h = (l) \times (w) \times (h) = (l)(w)(h), \text{ etc.}$$

Ratios and Proportions

1. Thinking proportionally is one of the most useful mathematical skills a student can develop. It is applicable to a wide variety of mathematical, occupational, and everyday settings.

2. A proportion is a set of equal ratios. The terms of a proportion—its means and extremes—are related mathematically: The product of the means is equal to the product of the extremes. Remind students that that is why it is important to keep the terms in proper order.

3. You can help students understand that corresponding sides of similar triangles are proportional. They can use that concept to solve shadow and proportion problems.

Chapter 7: Graphing

1. Emphasize to students the advantage of presenting data in graph form. Because graphs convey a lot of information quickly, it's easy to "get the picture." Graphs may also suggest patterns or trends in data over time.

2. Newspapers are a good source of graphs.

3. Have students think of examples of continuous and discontinuous data beyond those listed on page 136.

4. Give students practice in the skill of setting up axes on bar and line graphs. Prepare sets of data, and ask them to design and label appropriate axes, without necessarily graphing the data.

5. A common error in graphing is providing inconsistent units along the axes, as shown on page 139. Offer students the opportunity to practice making axes with consistent units.

6. You can facilitate students' understanding of dependent and independent variables by asking them to find examples of dependent and independent variables in everyday life. For example, weight might vary depending on food intake and exercise. In this case, weight is the dependent variable.

7. The idea of a best-fitting curve will make sense to students if you remind them of the error inherent in all measurements. Plotted points are not perfect, but they are only somewhat displaced from ideal data points. The best-fit curve joins these ideal points.

8. Students should be aware of the many different kinds of graphs they may encounter in various jobs.

9. Knowing how to extrapolate from known data is a powerful tool in answering questions such as how many plants to order for the nursery in the next growing season, how many bolts will be produced on the production line next week, how much flour to stock next month, and so on. You could ask students to suggest other examples of extrapolation.

PRACTICE ANSWERS

Note to the Teacher: Students' answers may differ slightly from those given here for a variety of reasons, such as the value of π used in calculations and methods of rounding.

Place Value in Numbers (page 1)

1. a. 200 + 10 + 5
   b. 8,000 + 300 + 70 + 8
   c. 60,000 + 3,000 + 400 + 70 + 9
   d. 800,000 + 10,000 + 3,000 + 700 + 20 + 1
   e. 10,000,000 + 400,000 + 40,000 + 2,000 + 100 + 70 + 9
   f. 50,000 + 70
   g. 0 + .40 + .05
   h. 0 + .03 + .007
   i. 2 + .30 + .08

Adding Whole Numbers (page 4)

1. a. 55
   b. 986
   c. 102
   d. 867
   e. 79
   f. 1,534
   g. 1,919
   h. 4,462
   i. 5,282
   j. 32,488
   k. 6,576

2. 895 bricks
3. 7,355 feet
4. 483 pounds
5. 143 mm
6. 1,264 bulbs
7. 6,224 tickets
8. 390 feet

9. Size A: 70
   Size B: 97
   Size C: 128
   Size D: 129
   Size E: 120
   Size F: 129

10. 3,216 m

Subtracting Whole Numbers (page 10)

1. a. 15
   b. 553
   c. 16
   d. 1,135
   e. 158

   f. 437
   g. 176
   h. 279
   i. 27,228
   j. 107,583

2. 9 mm
3. 16,853 transistors
4. 12,588 pounds
5. 58 pounds
6. 32 mm

7. 35 mm
8. 82 feet
9. 14 liters
10. 101 miles

Multiplying Whole Numbers (page 15)

1. a. 46
   b. 1,056
   c. 2,380
   d. 7,922

   e. 67,830
   f. 85,275
   g. 38,912
   h. 3,748,032

2. 360 hours
3. 4,950 nails
4. 2,376 spark plugs
   123,552 spark plugs
5. 2,200 carnations
   2,475 roses
   3,575 sprigs of greenery
6. 27,936 tiles
7. 4,080 reams
   2,040,000 sheets

8. Team 1: 1,008 transistors
   Team 2: 1,400 transistors
   Team 3: 1,540 transistors
   Team 4: 1,428 transistors
9. Team 1: 79,056 pounds
   Team 2: 63,504 pounds
   Team 3: 74,520 pounds
10. Elaine: 13,284 pounds
    Sam: 12,015 pounds
    Carlos: 13,095 pounds

Dividing Whole Numbers (page 22)

1. a. 23
   b. 27
   c. 35
   d. 92
   e. 68

   f. 113
   g. 99
   h. $23\frac{8}{35}$
   i. $8\frac{601}{989}$
   j. $62\frac{25}{32}$

2. $14 per hour
3. 34 pairs of shoes
4. 37 kilowatt hours
5. 42 files

6. 147 pounds/box
   $18\frac{3}{8}$ pounds/turkey
7. $1,021\frac{7}{46}$ gallons
8. 38 appetizers; 47 entrees;
   19 desserts; 59 beverages

9. 2,040 blanks

10. Vanna: $43\frac{29}{31}$ instruments;

Pat: $45\frac{10}{29}$ instruments;

Richard: $43\frac{4}{7}$ ($43\frac{16}{28}$)instruments

Fraction Terminology (page 29)

1. a. N = 2; D = 3
   b. N = 1; D = 6
   c. N = 4; D = 6

   d. N = 5; D = 2
   e. N = 2; D = 3
   f. N = 32; D = 15

   Proper fractions: a, c
   Mixed numbers: b, e
   Lowest terms: a, b, d, e, f

   Improper fractions: d, f
   Equivalent fractions: a, c

2. a. $1\frac{1}{2}$

   b. $2\frac{3}{5}$

   c. $3\frac{2}{7}$

   d. $12\frac{1}{5}$

   e. $18\frac{6}{7}$

3. a. $\frac{5}{4}$

   b. $\frac{36}{7}$

   c. $\frac{48}{5}$

   d. $\frac{64}{19}$

   e. $\frac{301}{13}$

4. a. $\frac{1}{4}$

   b. $\frac{4}{9}$

   c. OK

   d. $\frac{3}{5}$

   e. $\frac{3}{2}$

5. a. $x = 2$
   b. $x = 36$
   c. $x = 16$

   d. $x = 35$
   e. $x = 9$
   f. $x = 91$

Adding Fractions (page 33)

1. a. $\frac{11}{12}$

   b. $\frac{28}{45}$

   c. $\frac{13}{16}$

   d. $\frac{25}{24}$ ($1\frac{1}{24}$)

   e. $\frac{69}{64}$ ($1\frac{5}{64}$)

2. $29\frac{1}{2}$ inches

3. $30\frac{7}{8}$ feet

4. $12\frac{27}{64}$ inches

5. $5\frac{3}{8}$ inches

6. $11\frac{9}{16}$ feet

7. $3\frac{2}{3}$ sacks full

8. $21\frac{5}{6}$ Ω

9. $29\frac{7}{16}$ inches

10. $10\frac{3}{4}$ inches

Subtracting Fractions (page 37)

1. a. $\frac{1}{4}$

    b. $\frac{38}{63}$

    c. $\frac{7}{24}$

    d. $3\frac{1}{3}$

    e. $1\frac{5}{8}$

    f. $3\frac{3}{20}$

2. $12\frac{1}{2}$ feet

3. $\frac{7}{32}$ inch (one-half of $\frac{7}{16}$)

4. $\frac{7}{8}$ inch

5. $67\frac{1}{2}$ cords

6. $\frac{3}{64}$ " too thin

7. $1\frac{3}{8}$ inches

8. $2\frac{7}{8}$ inches

9. $35\frac{1}{2}$ yards

   $29\frac{5}{8}$ yards

   $22\frac{7}{8}$ yards

   $17\frac{1}{2}$ yards

10. Yes; $22\frac{1}{4}$ feet left over

Multiplying Fractions (page 40)

1. a. $\frac{2}{15}$

    b. $\frac{3}{10}$

    c. $\frac{1}{48}$

    d. 10

    e. $16\frac{17}{32}$

    f. $9\frac{1}{2}$

2. 74 feet

3. $26\frac{7}{8}$ pounds

   $40\frac{5}{16}$ pounds

   $5\frac{35}{36}$ pounds

4. $550\frac{1}{4}$ pounds

5. $10\frac{1}{2}$ cups flour

   $13\frac{1}{2}$ tsp vanilla extract

   9 tsp baking soda

   $1\frac{1}{8}$ cups raisins

   $7\frac{7}{8}$ cups sugar

   $1\frac{11}{16}$ cups nuts

   9 eggs

6. $151\frac{1}{3}$ pounds

7. $277\frac{7}{8}$ pounds

   $22\frac{1}{8}$ pounds short

8. $2\frac{1}{12}$ bags (about 2 bags)

   $76\frac{1}{24}$ pounds (about 76 pounds)

9. 30 ounces = $1\frac{7}{8}$ pounds

10. Tom $516\frac{9}{64}$ pounds

    Mikhail $508\frac{59}{64}$ pounds

    Turi $454\frac{25}{32}$ pounds

Dividing Fractions (page 44)

1. a. 3

    b. $\frac{14}{5}$

    c. $\frac{25}{24}$

    d. $\frac{1}{15}$

    e. $\frac{25}{57}$

    f. $\frac{75}{68}$

2. $15\frac{15}{19}$ (15 full solenoids)

3. $10\frac{5}{7}$ boards (10 boards)

4. 59 inches (4'11")

5. $3\frac{1}{16}$ inches

6. $51\frac{7}{19}$ boards (52 boards)

7. 50 minutes

    $65\frac{5}{13}$ minutes

    $72\frac{2}{9}$ minutes

    $85\frac{15}{61}$ minutes

    $76\frac{28}{47}$ minutes

8. (clockwise, from the top) 45 feet;

    $12\frac{1}{2}$ feet; 18 feet; 18 feet; 27 feet;

    $30\frac{1}{2}$ feet

Decimals and Percents (page 47)

1. a. 0.7

    b. 0.237

    c. 0.25

    d. 0.1875

    e. 0.26

    f. 0.4286

2. a. $\frac{7}{10}$

    b. $\frac{19}{20}$

    c. $\frac{1}{4}$

    d. $\frac{7}{1,000}$

    e. $\frac{139}{1,000}$

    f. $\frac{23}{50}$

3. a. 88%

    b. 80%

    c. 14%

    d. 83%

    e. 33%

    f. 47%

4. a. 29%

    b. 6%

    c. 99%

    d. 90%

    e. 78%

    f. 5%

5. a. 0.32

    b. 0.66

    c. 0.75

    d. 0.465

    e. 0.891

    f. 0.1786

6. a. $\frac{1}{4}$

    b. $\frac{2}{25}$

    c. $\frac{21}{50}$

    d. $\frac{5}{8}$

    e. $\frac{637}{1,000}$

    f. $\frac{147}{1,000}$

Adding Decimals (page 52)

1. a. 0.73
   b. 0.896
   c. 0.87
   d. 0.629
   e. 0.899
   f. 1.841
   g. 5.123
   h. 5.14
   i. 10.020
   j. 22.397
2. a. 5.6
   b. 0.5
   c. 9.3
   d. 17.5

3. a. 0.48
   b. 0.53
   c. 4.86
   d. 15.62
4. 57.7 mL
5. 1.45 inches
6. 9.3 inches
7. 5.95 inches
8. 0.1035 inches
9. 8.62 inches
10. 13.3299 centimeters

Subtracting Decimals (page 56)

1. a. 0.33
   b. 1.39
   c. 1.658
   d. 4.224
   e. 7.763
   f. 2.575
2. 1.28 inches
3. 87.4 inches
4. normal: 0.36 inch above the mat; light: 0.285 inch above the mat
5. 0.40 inch
6. No. It must be reduced by another 0.063 inch.
7. 249.4 gallons; 229.2 gallons; 198.8 gallons; 238.8 gallons; 213.6 gallons
8. 4.450 inches; 3.8625 inches; 3.1030 inches; 3.01425 inches
9. 92.5 mL; 86.25 mL; 54.7 mL; 49.25 mL; 26.86 mL; 0.785 mL
10. 0.0149 inch; 0.0150 inch; 0.0149 inch; 0.0149 inch

Multiplying Decimals (page 60)

1. a. 0.06
   b. 0.858
   c. 74.26
   d. 2.24

   e. 33.108
   f. 1,200
   g. 140.148
   h. 648.648

2. $96.25; $481.25
3. AB: 11"
   BC: 6.875"
   CD: 9.625"
   DE: 3.4375"
   EF: 15.8125"
   FA: 13.0625"
4. 1,404 pounds;
   21,060 pounds

5. A: 384 oz; B: 748 oz; C: 1,289.25 oz;
   Total 2,421.25 oz
6. 1,062.5 cm/minute
7. (1) 210 feet; (2) 345 feet; (3) 615 feet;
   (4) 1,950 feet; (5) 7,545 feet
8. (1) 1,200 feet; (2) 3,264 feet; (3) 4,200 feet;
   (4) 5,256 feet
9. 334.7 cm

Dividing Decimals (page 64)

1. a. 5.6
    b. 5.7
    c. 1.24
    d. 8.41
    e. 14.28
    f. 5.97
    g. 0.05 (0.052)
    h. 0.08 (0.075)
    i. 0.12
2. 6 (5.45) pieces
3. 120 minutes (2 hours)

4. 423 or 424 (423.7) sheets
5. 112 (112.16) wires
6. 18 threads
7. 494 pins
8. 2,545 (2,544.12) layers
9. 618 hours; 8.7 workers
10. 82,144 complete sections. The exact answer,
    82,144.9, includes a partial section
    (0.9 × 0.8765 cm = 0.78885 cm waste).

Operations With Fractions and Decimals (page 67)

1. a. 0.6
    b. 0.076
    c. 5.793
    d. 0.800
    e. 0.762
    f. 3.358

2. $2,873.81
3. $14.08
4. 4.14 kilograms
5. 27.67 square yards
6. $11\frac{1}{4}$ pieces

Percents *(page 71)*

1. a. 60%
    b. 42.1%
    c. 75.5%
    d. 34.4%
    e. 133.3%
2. a. 15
    b. 3.8
    c. 8.19
    d. 4.41
    e. 0.0005463
3. a. $50
    b. $112.50
    c. $513.34
    d. $175.83

4. 3.47% defective: Henry gets the deduction.
5. March 121%; yes; April 118%; no; May 118%; no; June 128%; yes
6. 82.3%; 95.9%; 75.2%
7. Meyer's 19.6%; Black Cat 16.3%; Honest 21.9%; Sunshine 15.7%
8. copper 23.2 grams; zinc 28.5 grams; antimony 6.8 grams
9. 7.3%
10. clockwise from the top: $26\frac{1}{4}$ feet; $21\frac{1}{8}$ feet; $9\frac{5}{8}$ feet; $3\frac{1}{2}$ feet; $16\frac{5}{8}$ feet; $18\frac{3}{8}$ feet

Roots and Powers *(page 77)*

1. 121
2. 17.64
3. 0.20
4. 1,728
5. 9.26
6. 1.73
7. 9
8. 15.59
9. 0.81
10. 0.08

Linear, Angular, and Circular Measurement *(page 81)*

1. 14.6 in
2. 98.6 cm
3. 2,660 ft
4. 292 in; 297 in
5. 116.2 ft
6. 1,681.5 ft
7. 53.42 cm
8. $212\frac{1}{2}$ ft

Area *(page 85)*

1. a. 289 cm²
    b. 9.24 ft²
    c. 26.4 in²
    d. 83.4 cm²
    e. 1,882.4 ft²
    f. 29,240.5 cm²
    g. 375.8 ft²
    h. 64.9 in²
    i. 4574.2 cm²

2. 1,104 ft²; 3 gallons; $53.85
3. 615.44 in²
4. 1,371.6 cm²
5. 2,007 bricks; $903.15
6. 23.1 in²
7. 1,566.2 ft²; 3,155.7 ft²; 4,721.9 ft²
8. *A:* 7,040 ft²; *B:* 7,040 ft²; *C:* 9,384 ft²; *D:* 8,316 ft²; *E:* 7,040 ft²; *F:* 7,040 ft²; *G:* 8,320 ft²; *H:* 6,912 ft²

Volume (page 92)

1. a. 98.97 in³
   b. 140,608 cm³
   c. 893.28 in³
   d. 0.94 m³
   e. 24,306 ft³
2. 24.6 gal

3. 197.04 ft³
4. 15.6 mm³
5. Answers may vary slightly depending on the conversion factor used. About 420 yd³ (11,319 ft³)

Measurement (page 97)

1. All answers are given $\pm\frac{1}{16}$"

   a. *GD*: $1\frac{9}{16}$"; *DE*: 2";

      EF: $2\frac{7}{16}$"; *FG*: $2\frac{1}{2}$"

   b. *HJ*: 2"; *IH*: $2\frac{3}{4}$";

      JK: 4"; *IK*: $3\frac{5}{16}$"; *IJ*: $3\frac{15}{15}$"

2. a. 6" to $6\frac{1}{2}$"; $\frac{1}{2}$"

   b. $8\frac{5}{8}$" to $8\frac{7}{8}$"; $\frac{1}{4}$"

   c. 6.23" to 6.27"; 0.04"

   d. 4.70 cm to 4.80 cm; 0.10 cm

   e. 2.638" to 2.640"; 0.002"

   f. 1.038 cm to 1.042 cm; 0.004 cm

   g. 2.036" to 2.046"; 0.010"

   h. 0.789 mm to 0.795 mm; 0.006 mm

3. 65 mL; 7.2 mL; 4.55 mL
4. a. 3,421 ccf
   b. 4,087.2 ccf
5. a. 6,442 kwh
   b. 1,890 kwh

Measuring Systems (page 105)

1. a. 24 in
   b. 2.5 lb
   c. 10.76 qt
   d. 670.95 gal
   e. 13.14 yd
   f. 0.0405 ft
   g. 0.509 pt
   h. 212.9 in³

2. 33 pt
3. yes; loaded weight is 19,800 lb (9.9 tons).
4. 52.7 gal
5. 630 1-pt canisters
6. no; $65\frac{5}{8}$ yd needed; short by $10\frac{5}{8}$ yd
7. 133 rolls
8. 8 in; 24 points

The Metric System (page 108)

1. a. 500 cg
    b. 0.863 g
    c. 2,350 mm
    d. 74,580 mL
    e. 47.9 cc
    f. 1.8734 km
    g. 583 mm
    h. 427 mm

2. 14.07 L
3. 938.8 m
4. 8.875 kg
5. 4.055 L
6. $16.93 (18.3 kg)
7. 12.72 g
8. 37.43 km

Measuring Devices (page 113)

1. a. 6.19 mm
    b. 2.77 mm
    c. 8.02 mm
    d. 3.61 mm

2. a. 130.62 mm; 5.143 in
    b. 71.78 mm; 2.826 in
    c. 204.14 mm; 8.037 in
    d. 11.96 mm; 0.471 in

3. a. 74.5°
    b. 65.0°
    c. 40.5°
    d. 35.0°
    e. 126.0°
    f. 60.09°
    g. 118.0°
    h. 87.0°

Mathematical Formulas (page 121)

1. a. $i = \dfrac{V}{r}$

    b. $r = \dfrac{P}{i^2}$

    c. $f = \dfrac{c}{\lambda}$

    d. $v_0 = v - at$

    e. $r = \dfrac{12C}{\pi D}$

    f. $A = \dfrac{v_0 T}{2\pi}$

2. 3,092 ft

3. 90 ft
4. 44.7 ft
5. 9.6°C
6. 2,000 lb
7. 35.2 amp
8. 18.5 ft/min

Ratios and Proportions (page 128)

1. Answers may vary slightly, depending on student measurements.

   a. 1.13

   b. 0.53

   c. 0.40

   d. 0.39

2. A: 33:1; B: 24:1; C: 28.7:1;

   D: 16:1; E: 19.7:1

3. Set A: 2:1; Set B: 3:1; Set C: 3.5:1;

   Set D: 4.75:1; Set E: 4.4:1

4. r_1r_2, 0.2:1; r_1r_3, 3.33:1;

   r_1r_4, 2.31:1; r_2r_3, 16.67:1;

   r_2r_4, 11.57:1; r_3r_4, 0.69:1

5. *A:* $\frac{3}{1}$

   B: $\frac{8}{3}$

   C: $\frac{11}{3}$

   D: $\frac{9}{5}$

6. 3001: $\frac{25}{12}$; 2.08:1

   3008: $\frac{75}{23}$; 3.26:1

   3017: $\frac{4}{1}$; 4:1

   3029: $\frac{170}{13}$; 13.08:1

   3085: $\frac{1,170}{93}$; 12.58:1

7. 508 reams

8. 667 lb

9. 1,125 cc catsup

   168.75 cc Tabasco sauce

   1,406.25 cc clam juice

   78.75 cc Worcestershire sauce

   225 cc lemon juice

10. Circuit 1: 22.4 ohms

    Circuit 2: 26.5 ohms

    Circuit 3: 20.0 ohms

    Circuit 4: 34.6 ohms

Graphing (page 135)

1. a.

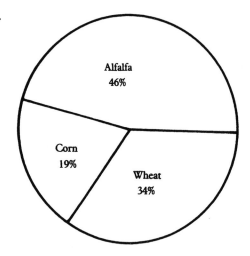

b.

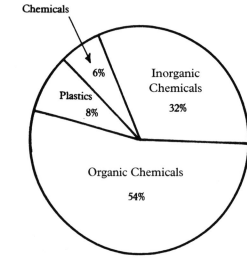

c.

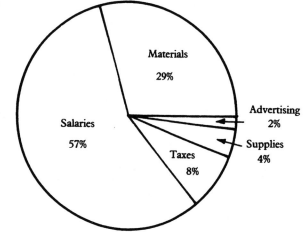

d.

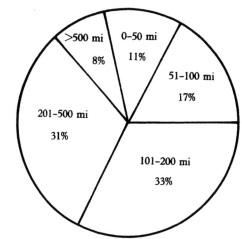

e.

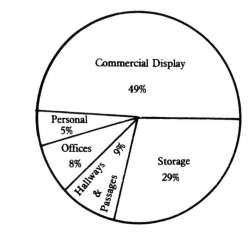

2. 0–$25,000: 42

$25,001–$50,000: 65;

$50,001–$75,000: 16;

$75,001–$100,000: 7;

$100,000+: 2

3. Best seller: $\frac{1}{2}$ ", 20,754

Poorest seller: $\frac{1}{8}$ ", 4,178

4.   a.

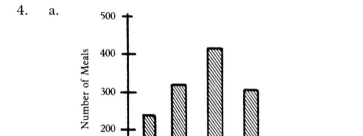

b.

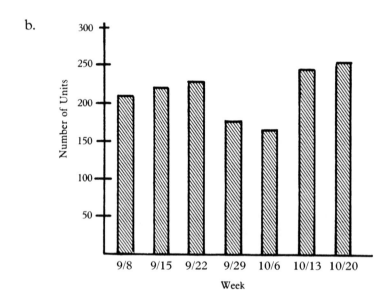

c.

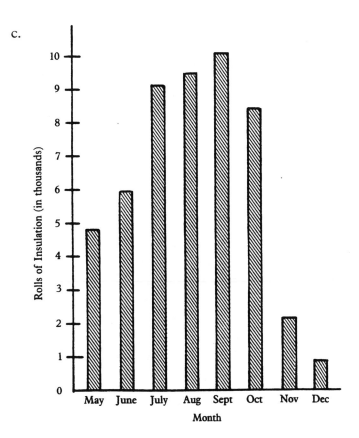

d.

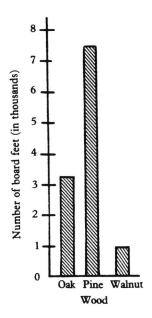

e.

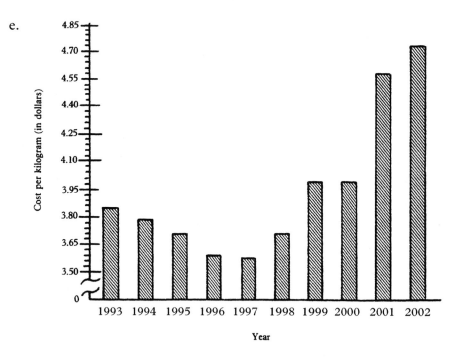

5. Stainless steel, 1,430°C;

   difference 166°C

6.   a. 52 hours

     b. 106 hours

     c. June, July

7. a.

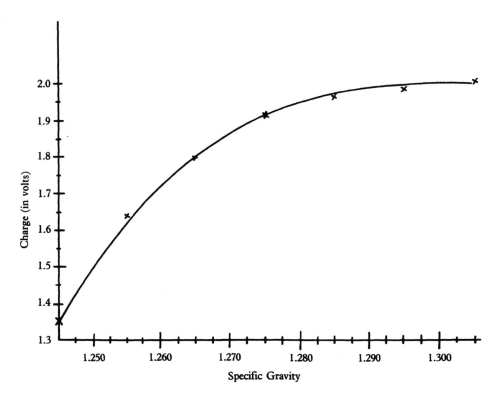

b.

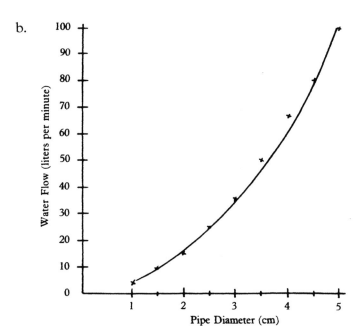

c.

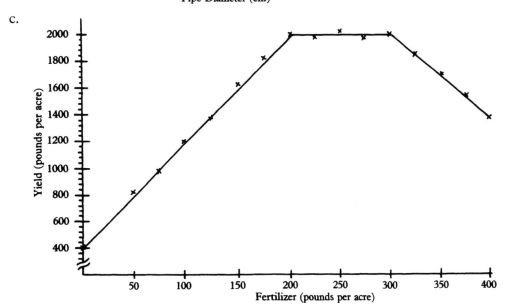

8. a. Highest temperature: 3 min; lowest temperature: 9 min

    b. 5 min

    c. 2,200°C

9. a. 22%; 6%

    b. 32 ft; 12 ft

    c. 4%

10. a. 1955: 32,000 tons; 1970: 70,000 tons; 1985: 70,000 tons; 2000: 88,000 tons

    b. about 1962; about 1995; has not yet reached this level

    c. Answer depends on the type of extrapolation made. A straight-line extrapolation gives 98,000 tons for 2005; 108,000 tons for 2010; and 118,000 tons for 2015. One could also predict that supplies of coal will be exhausted or that greater finds will be made, resulting in either smaller or larger predictions.

Chapter 1: Pretest

1. Express each of the following numbers using numerals.

    a. six thousand four hundred seventy-three
    b. three hundred nineteen thousand four hundred seven

2. Express each of the following numbers in words.

    a. 10,725
    b. 917

3. Perform each of the indicated additions.

    a. 304 + 625
    b. 8,139 + 1,490
    c. 2,876 + 38,495

4. Perform each of the indicated subtractions.

    a. 795 – 321
    b. 6,442 – 5,813
    c. 2,015 – 873

5. Perform each of the indicated multiplications.

    a. 23 × 7
    b. 148 × 15
    c. 264 × 87

6. Perform each of the indicated divisions.

    a. 168 ÷ 6
    b. 1,786 ÷ 47
    c. 5,186 ÷ 32

7. Maury purchases four pieces of cloth with the following lengths: 18 ft, 27 ft, 75 ft, and 63 ft. What is the total length of the four pieces of cloth?

8. Francesco cuts a 28-inch piece of solder off a roll 110 inches long. How much solder remains on the roll?

9. Each of the 138 workers on the Clippo Company's production line uses an average of 45 ounces of lubricating oil per day. What is the total amount of oil used by all workers on the line?

10. Each person at Bella's editorial service is expected to read the same number of manuscript pages each day. How many pages should each expect to read if there are 17 readers and 3,672 pages to be read?

Chapter 1: Posttest

1. Express each of the following numbers using numerals.

    a. five thousand three hundred ninety-eight

    b. seven hundred eighty-three thousand ninety-two

2. Express each of the following numbers in words.

    a. 602

    b. 37,211

3. Perform each of the indicated additions.

    a. 273 + 514

    b. 4,652 + 3,867

    c. 26,847 + 7,815

4. Perform each of the indicated subtractions.

    a. 697 − 146

    b. 5,813 − 4,784

    c. 6,102 − 845

5. Perform each of the indicated multiplications.

    a. 34 × 6

    b. 315 × 26

    c. 826 × 39

6. Perform each of the indicated divisions.

    a. 216 ÷ 9

    b. 1,634 ÷ 38

    c. 5,084 ÷ 23

7. The members of Jan's production team have turned out the following numbers of units this week: 58, 69, 174, 138, and 217. What is the total number of units produced by the team this week?

8. Of the 681 calves born on Phan's farm this year, 285 were sold at auction. How many of the calves remain on Phan's farm?

9. Each facing brick used on the new Hochstetler building weighs 875 grams. What is the total weight, in kilograms, of the 2,850 bricks used on the building? (1 kilogram = 1,000 grams.)

10. A carboy holding 45 liters of acid has to be emptied into 135-milliliter containers. How many such containers can be completely filled? (1 liter = 1,000 milliliters.)

Chapter 2: Pretest

1. Reduce each of the following fractions to lowest terms.

   a. $\frac{18}{24}$

   b. $\frac{90}{126}$

   c. $\frac{72}{180}$

2. Change each of the following mixed numbers to an improper fraction.

   a. $2\frac{3}{5}$

   b. $5\frac{2}{7}$

   c. $16\frac{2}{11}$

3. Change each of the following improper fractions to a mixed number.

   a. $\frac{18}{5}$

   b. $\frac{200}{3}$

   c. $\frac{374}{16}$

4. Change each of the following fractions to an equivalent fraction with the numerator or denominator given. Solve for x.

   a. $\frac{2}{7} = \frac{x}{35}$

   b. $\frac{3}{8} = \frac{24}{x}$

   c. $\frac{11}{x} = \frac{121}{275}$

5. Perform each of the indicated operations.

   a. $\frac{4}{9} + \frac{3}{11}$

   b. $2\frac{3}{8} + 1\frac{5}{6}$

   c. $\frac{10}{11} - \frac{2}{3}$

   d. $6\frac{1}{5} - 1\frac{2}{9}$

6. Perform each of the indicated operations.

   a. $\frac{5}{9} \times \frac{3}{16}$

   b. $4\frac{2}{3} \times 3\frac{1}{6}$

   c. $8\frac{2}{3} \div 1\frac{1}{4}$

7. Three bars of the lengths listed below are welded together. What is the total length of the welded bar?

   section 1: $8\frac{3}{4}$ in;   section 2: $16\frac{7}{8}$ in;   section 3: $25\frac{1}{2}$ in

8. Zeke saws a $2\frac{5}{6}$-ft board from a piece of stock $14\frac{1}{2}$ ft long. How much stock remains?

9. Each can of tar Tomas uses weighs $8\frac{3}{4}$ lb. What is the weight of $4\frac{1}{2}$ cans of tar?

10. A wall $12\frac{1}{2}$ ft wide is painted with alternate black and white stripes. Each stripe is $6\frac{1}{4}$ in wide. How many stripes are there on the wall?

Chapter 2: Posttest

1. Reduce each of the following fractions to lowest terms.

   a. $\frac{96}{120}$

   b. $\frac{64}{288}$

   c. $\frac{90}{165}$

2. Change each of the following mixed numbers to an improper fraction.

   a. $3\frac{2}{7}$

   b. $4\frac{3}{8}$

   c. $18\frac{5}{9}$

3. Change each of the following improper fractions to a mixed number.

   a. $\frac{16}{3}$

   b. $\frac{67}{4}$

   c. $\frac{290}{14}$

4. Change each of the following fractions to an equivalent fraction with the numerator or denominator given. Solve for x.

   a. $\frac{3}{5} = \frac{x}{60}$

   b. $\frac{4}{11} = \frac{24}{x}$

   c. $\frac{8}{x} = \frac{72}{117}$

5. Perform each of the indicated operations.

   a. $\frac{3}{5} + \frac{7}{12}$

   b. $3\frac{2}{5} + 5\frac{2}{9}$

   c. $\frac{9}{10} - \frac{1}{7}$

   d. $6\frac{2}{5} - 3\frac{7}{8}$

6. Perform each of the indicated operations.

   a. $\frac{4}{7} \times \frac{2}{15}$

   c. $6\frac{1}{3} \div 4\frac{3}{4}$

   b. $3\frac{2}{7} \times 9\frac{5}{6}$

   d. $1\frac{2}{5} \div 14\frac{1}{2}$

7. Charlene welds together four lengths of pipe: $13\frac{1}{2}$", $28\frac{3}{4}$", $9\frac{7}{8}$", and $15\frac{5}{8}$". What is the total length of the welded piece?

8. How much remains of a pipe originally $75\frac{3}{4}$ ft long after Elmira cuts off a piece $26\frac{7}{8}$ ft long?

9. Fern harvests $21\frac{7}{8}$ bushels of apples, each weighing an average of $48\frac{1}{2}$ pounds. What is the total weight of the apples harvested?

10. How many pieces of ribbon, each $8\frac{3}{4}$ in long, can Ken cut from a 15-yard roll of ribbon?

Basic Occupational Math

Chapter 3: Pretest

1. Make each of the following conversions. Round to the nearest ten thousandth.

    a. Convert to a common fraction: (1) 0.375 (2) 0.562 (3) 26%

    b. Convert to a decimal: (1) $\frac{3}{16}$ (2) $\frac{4}{29}$ (3) 71%

    c. Convert to a percent: (1) $\frac{2}{5}$ (2) $\frac{13}{30}$ (3) 0.18

2. Perform each of the following indicated additions.

    a. 0.347 + 0.512   b. 1.8793 + 6.426   c. 12.04 + 8.589

3. Perform each of the following indicated subtractions.

    a. 4.87 − 2.36   b. 9.712 − 4.386   c. 12.05 − 10.627

4. Perform each of the following indicated multiplications.

    a. 1.2 × 2.4   b. 3.74 × 2.6   c. 4.19 × 5.26

5. Perform each of the following indicated divisions. Round answers, where necessary, to the nearest ten thousandth.

    a. 2.99 ÷ 2.3   b. 25.85 ÷ 4.7   c. 16.83 ÷ 9.64

6. Solve each of the following problems. Round answers, where necessary, to the nearest hundredth.

    a. What percent of 18 is 4?   c. What is 35% of 180?

    b. What percent is 19 of 22?   d. What is 42% of 29.8?

7. What is the total width of a fabric panel prepared by JoAnn if it consists of four segments whose widths are 1.47 m, 2.85 m, 3.06 m, and 2.59 m?

8. Terrell draws off 78.47 mL of solution from a container that holds 309.50 mL of the solution. How much remains in the container?

9. In an experiment, Randy uses 16.875 mL of a solution that weighs 2.53 g per mL. What is the weight of the solution used in the experiment, rounded to the nearest hundredth?

10. Each sheet of steel in a stack 259.0 cm high is 1.75 cm thick. How many sheets are there in the pile?

Chapter 3: Posttest

1. Make each of the following conversions. Round to the nearest ten thousandth.

    a. Convert to a common fraction: (1) 0.875 (2) 0.684 (3) 38%

    b. Convert to a decimal: (1) $\frac{9}{16}$ (2) $\frac{11}{35}$ (3) 56%

    c. Convert to a percent: (1) $\frac{4}{5}$ (2) $\frac{9}{55}$ (3) 0.39

2. Perform each of the following indicated additions.

    a. 0.158 + 0.621   b. 2.385 + 5.667   c. 23.9 + 8.742

3. Perform each of the following indicated subtractions.

    a. 5.96 − 2.35   b. 12.412 − 8.628   c. 25.02 − 11.848

4. Perform each of the following indicated multiplications.

    a. 1.3 × 3.2   b. 4.58 × 3.4   c. 6.85 × 4.37

5. Perform each of the following indicated divisions. Round answers, where necessary, to the nearest ten thousandth.

    a. 5.04 ÷ 2.1   b. 25.16 ÷ 6.8   c. 20.46 ÷ 6.97

6. Solve each of the following problems. Round answers, where necessary, to the nearest hundredth.

    a. What percent of 22 is 5?   c. What is 21% of 165?

    b. What percent is 17 of 28?   d. What is 39% of 78.5?

7. Ozzie makes a solution by mixing three liquids whose volumes are 28.5 mL, 36.9 mL, and 147.8 mL. What is the total volume of the final solution?

8. The total thickness of a book is 4.62 cm. How thick are the two covers together if the pages themselves make up 4.39 cm of the book?

9. What is Rollie's paycheck, rounded to the nearest cent, for a week in which he worked $38\frac{3}{8}$ hr if his hourly pay is $13.69?

10. A punch machine turns out metal keys 0.958 cm wide. How many such keys can be cut from a piece of stock 250 cm long?

Chapter 4: Pretest

1. Find each of the powers.

    a. $(8)^2$ b. $(23.7)^2$ c. $(9)^3$ d. $(1.6)^3$

2. Find each of the roots. Round answers to the nearest hundredth where necessary.

    a. $\sqrt{169}$ b. $\sqrt{62.14}$ c. $\sqrt{34,596}$ d. $\sqrt[3]{125}$

3. Find each of the lengths requested in the following problems. Round answers to the nearest hundredth where necessary.

    a. The perimeter of a rectangle whose width is 13.7 inches and whose length is 30.9 inches

    b. The circumference of a circle whose radius is 3.29 feet

4. Find each of the areas requested in the following problems. Round answers to the nearest tenth where necessary.

    a. A square whose side is 11.7 cm

    b. A triangle whose base is 8.6 feet and whose altitude is 10.9 feet

    c. A circle with a diameter of 7.43 meters

5. Find each of the volumes requested in the following problems. Round answers to the nearest hundredth where necessary.

    a. A rectangular block with dimensions 3.8 cm by 18.6 cm by 34.9 cm

    b. A cone 17.4 ft high with a base of radius 1.06 ft

    c. A sphere whose diameter is 16.4 cm

6. What is the distance around Max's circular patio if the distance across the patio is 125 feet?

7. Cho must paint a fence 213 feet long and 5 feet 4 inches high. What is the area of the fence to be painted? Round your answer to the nearest foot.

8. What is the volume of a cylindrical tank that is 34.5 ft high and 12.5 ft across? Round your answer to the nearest tenth.

Chapter 4: Posttest

1. Find each of the powers.

    a. $(14)^2$ b. $(61.4)^2$ c. $(11)^3$ d. $(2.3)^3$

2. Find each of the roots. Round answers to the nearest hundredth where necessary.

    a. $\sqrt{256}$ b. $\sqrt{129.43}$ c. $\sqrt{24,400}$ d. $\sqrt[3]{43}$

3. Find each of the lengths requested in the following problems. Round answers to the nearest hundredth where necessary.

    a. The perimeter of a rectangle whose width is $16\frac{3}{4}$ inches and whose length is $5\frac{1}{8}$ inches

    b. The circumference of a circle whose radius is 6.74 inches

4. Find each of the areas requested in the following problems. Round answers to the nearest tenth where necessary.

    a. A rectangle with a width of $4\frac{3}{4}$ inches and a length of $9\frac{1}{8}$ inches

    b. A trapezoid with bases of 86.9 cm and 98.5 cm and an altitude of 13.7 cm

    c. A circle with a diameter of 13.69 cm

5. Find each of the volumes requested in the following problems. Give your answers as a mixed number or a decimal rounded to the nearest hundredth where necessary.

    a. A cube that is 6.795 cm on a side

    b. A cylinder with a height of $42\frac{3}{4}$ inches, whose base has a radius of $1\frac{3}{4}$ inches

    c. A sphere whose diameter is $4\frac{3}{8}$ inches

6. Connie ties a stack of aluminum sheets together with two bands of steel, one wrapped along the long dimension of the stack and one along the wide dimension. Each sheet of aluminum is $2\frac{1}{2}$ feet long, 8 inches wide, and $\frac{1}{8}$ inch thick. How much steel banding is needed to wrap a stack of 50 sheets?

7. A machine punches out 100 circles of brass, each with a diameter of 1.375 cm, from a sheet of brass 12 cm by 15 cm. How much scrap remains from the sheet?

8. The top of a building Lee is designing has the shape of a pyramid 15.82 feet high with a square base 26.91 feet on a side. What is the volume of this pyramid?

Name _____ Date _____

Chapter 5: Pretest

1. With measuring devices provided by your instructor, find

   a. The length of the line at the right, in inches _____

   b. The length of the line at the right, in centimeters _____

   c. The size of the two angles at the right, to the greatest precision allowed with your measuring device

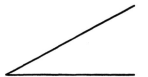 

2. Determine the upper limit, the lower limit, and the range of tolerances for each of the following measurements.

   a. $6\frac{3}{4}" \pm \frac{1}{2}"$

   b. $2.178" \pm 0.002"$

   c. $4.341 \text{ mm} \begin{array}{l} + 0.001 \text{ mm} \\ - 0.003 \text{ mm} \end{array}$

3. Record the volume, weight, and meter readings shown below.

   a.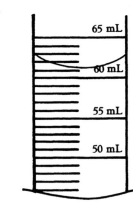

   b.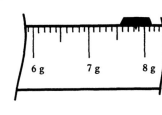

   c.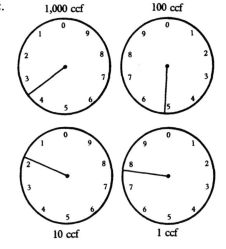

4. Convert each of the following measurements to the units given.

   a. 4.73 qt = _____ gal

   b. 1,623 ft = _____ mi

   c. 0.843 lb = _____ oz

   d. 1.0583 mi = _____ in

   e. 18.3 cm = _____ m

   f. 0.68 kg = _____ g

   g. 218.5 mL = _____ L

   h. 1.873.8 cg = _____ kg

Chapter 5: Posttest

1. With measuring devices provided by your instructor, find

   a. the length of the line at the right, in inches. _____

   b. the length of the line at the right, in centimeters. _____

   c. the size of the two angles at the right, to the greatest precision allowed with your measuring device.

2. Determine the upper limit, the lower limit, and the range of tolerances for each measurement listed below.

   a. $7\frac{3}{8}" \pm \frac{3}{8}"$

   b. $1.659" \pm 0.003"$

   c. $7.298 \text{ mm} \begin{array}{l} + 0.004 \text{ mm} \\ - 0.001 \text{ mm} \end{array}$

3. Record the volume, weight, and meter readings shown below.

   a.

   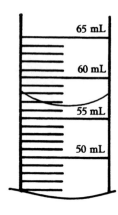

   b.

   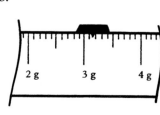

   c.

   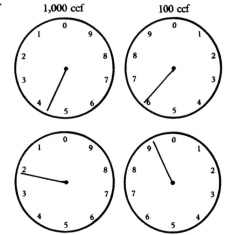

4. Convert each of the following measurements to the units given.

   a. 2.31 gal = _____ qt

   b. 6.79 yd = _____ ft

   c. 403.8 oz = _____ lb

   d. 3.486 pt = _____ gal

   e. 1.76 m = _____ cm

   f. 823.4 g = _____ kg

   g. 0.0645 L = _____ mL

   h. 1.487 kg = _____ cg

Chapter 6: Pretest

1. Solve each of the following formulas for the underlined letter.

    a. $C = 2\pi \underline{r}$ b. $A = \frac{1}{2} b\underline{h}$

2. Find the diameter of a circle whose circumference is 14 feet.

3. The longer side of Van's rectangular field is 1,240 feet in length. How long is the shorter side if a fence 3,540 feet just encloses the field?

4. The wire Nadia is testing in her laboratory stretches when weights are placed on it according to the formula

    $$l = l_0 + 0.000865 \, m$$

    where l is the length (in centimeters) of the wire with a weight on it, l_0 is the length without the weight (in centimeters), and m is the weight (in grams) placed on the wire. What weight must be placed on a wire that is originally 186.5 cm long to make it stretch to a length of 186.9 cm?

5. Express each of the following pairs of numbers as a ratio, the first number to the second number. Reduce each ratio to its lowest terms. Also express the ratio in the format $a : 1$.

    a. $8 : 4$ b. $\frac{1}{6}$ foot : 6 inches   c. 17.5 cm : 4.2 cm

6. Calculate the value of x in each of the following proportions.

    a. $\frac{3}{7} = \frac{4}{x}$ b. $\frac{1.5}{2.7} = \frac{x}{6.3}$ c. $\frac{21.5}{x} = \frac{4.8}{9.3}$

7. Roseanne operates a piledriver. The machine sinks a steel post 0.15 cm each time a force of 2,500 pounds is applied. What force is needed to sink the same post a distance of 0.25 cm in a single blow?

8. Juan bakes a cake for six people. The recipe calls for 15 g of baking soda. How much baking soda should he add to a larger cake intended for 75 people?

Chapter 6: Posttest

1. Solve each of the following formulas for the underlined letter.

   a. $p = k\underline{d}h$

   b. $A = 6\underline{s}^2$

2. What is the height of a cylinder whose base is 6 inches in diameter and whose volume is 1,639 cubic inches?

3. Olive places one drop of adhesive between two plastic sheets, each 25 cm by 35 cm in size. The drop contains 1.500 cubic centimeters of adhesive. The adhesive spreads out and completely covers the space between the two sheets. What is the thickness of the layer of adhesive?

4. Jamie's test car accelerates from 35 miles per hour to 60 miles per hour in 4.2 seconds. To calculate the car's acceleration, Jamie uses the formula $v = v_0 + at$, where v_0 is the original speed (in miles per hour), v is the final velocity (in miles per hour), a is the acceleration (in miles per hour per second), and t is the time (in seconds). What is the car's acceleration?

5. Express each of the following pairs of numbers as a ratio of the first number to the second number. Reduce each ratio to its lowest terms. Also express the ratio in the format $a : 1$.

   a. $72 : 18$

   b. $\frac{1}{16}$ mile : 440 feet

   c. 252 mm : 72 mm

6. Calculate the value of x in each of the following proportions.

   a. $\frac{7}{11} = \frac{x}{5}$

   b. $\frac{4.7}{13.6} = \frac{21.3}{x}$

   c. $\frac{x}{22.7} = \frac{9.04}{5.16}$

7. Orlando's paint crew normally uses 2.5 gallons of primer to cover 350 square feet of new siding. How many gallons of primer should he buy to paint a house that has 2,000 square feet of new siding?

8. Pho's monthly budget for the salaries of 13 people who work for him is $15,585. What should he budget for salaries if he adds 5 new employees at the same rate of pay?

Chapter 7: Pretest

1. From the circle graph at the right, calculate the number of employees engaged in each type of work at the Jow-La Company. Round your answers to the nearest whole number.

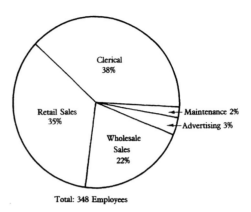

Clerical 38%

Retail Sales 35%

Maintenance 2%

Advertising 3%

Wholesale Sales 22%

Total: 348 Employees

2. The number of new homes sold by Rhea's real estate firm over the last six months is shown below. Make a bar graph that represents these data.

   March: 36   May: 41   July: 59

   April: 45   June: 52   August: 68

3. The melting point of a certain alloy varies depending on the percent of antimony used in making the alloy. The table below shows this variation. Construct a line graph that represents this information.

Percent Antimony	5%	7.5%	10%	12.5%	15%	17.5%	20%	22.5%
Melting Point (°C)	420	408	400	384	372	361	344	332

4. The line graph below shows the electricity used by the residents of Culver City during a typical 12-hour period. Answer the following questions about this graph.

   a. At what time of day was the most electrical energy used?

   b. How much electrical energy was used at 12 noon on this day? at 9 A.M.?

   c. Predict electrical-energy use at 6 A.M.; at 10 P.M.

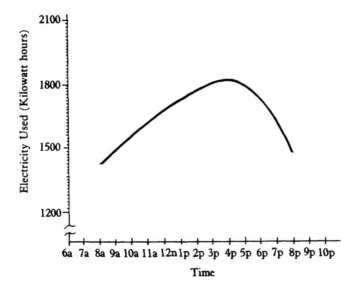

Chapter 7: Posttest

1. Construct a circle graph that represents the following distribution of students in the San Felipe School District. Round your answers to the nearest whole number.

Hispanic	379	African American	297
Asian	402	Caucasian	511
Filipino	168	Other	26

2. The bar graph at the right shows the number of cars sold by the sales team at Honest Hedda's Used Car Lot last year. Answer the following questions about the graph.

   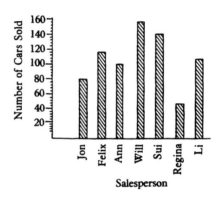

   a. Which salesperson sold the most cars last year? How many cars did that person sell?

   b. Which salesperson sold the fewest cars last year? How many cars did that person sell?

   c. How many salespersons exceeded Honest Hedda's goal of 100 cars sold per person last year? Who were they?

3. The graph at the right shows the population of West Vancouver Heights since 1945. Answer the following questions about this graph.

   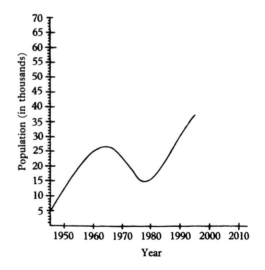

   a. What was the population of West Vancouver Heights in 1945? In 1960? In 1975? In 1990?

   b. In which years has the population fallen to between 25,000 and 35,000?

   c. What population would you predict for West Vancouver Heights in the year 2005? The year 2010?

4. Lola counts the number of bacterial colonies growing on a petri dish over a 24-hour period at constant temperature. Her data are shown below. Make a line graph that represents these data.

Time	Number of Bacterial Colonies	Time	Number of Bacterial Colonies
7:00 A.M.	115	3:00 P.M.	210
9:00 A.M.	120	5:00 P.M.	265
11:00 A.M.	149	7:00 P.M.	363
1:00 P.M.	169	9:00 P.M.	467

TEST ANSWERS

Chapter 1 Pretest

1. a. 6,473
   b. 319,407

2. a. ten thousand seven hundred twenty-five
   b. nine hundred seventeen

3. a. 929
   b. 9,629
   c. 41,371

4. a. 474
   b. 629
   c. 1,142

5. a. 161
   b. 2,220
   c. 22,968

6. a. 28
   b. 38
   c. $162\frac{1}{16}$ ($162\frac{2}{32}$) (or 162.0625)

7. 183 ft (61 yds.)

8. 82 in

9. 6,210 oz

10. 216 pages

Chapter 1 Posttest

1. a. 5,398
   b. 783,092

2. a. six hundred two
   b. thirty-seven thousand two hundred eleven

3. a. 787
   b. 8,519
   c. 34,662

4. a. 551
   b. 1,029
   c. 5,257

5. a. 204
   b. 8,190
   c. 32,214

6. a. 24
   b. 43
   c. $221\frac{1}{23}$ (or 221.0434)

7. 656 units

8. 396 calves

9. 2,493.75 kg

10. 333 ($333\frac{1}{3}$) containers

Chapter 2 Pretest

1. a. $\frac{3}{4}$

   b. $\frac{5}{7}$

   c. $\frac{2}{5}$

2. a. $\frac{13}{5}$

   b. $\frac{37}{7}$

   c. $\frac{178}{11}$

3. a. $3\frac{3}{5}$

   b. $66\frac{2}{3}$

   c. $23\frac{3}{8}$

4. a. $x = 10$

   b. $x = 64$

   c. $x = 25$

5. a. $\frac{71}{99}$

   b. $4\frac{5}{24}$

   c. $\frac{8}{33}$

   d. $4\frac{44}{45}$

6. a. $\frac{5}{48}$

   b. $14\frac{7}{9}$

   c. $6\frac{14}{15}$

7. $51\frac{1}{8}$ in

8. $11\frac{5}{12}$ ft

9. $39\frac{3}{8}$ lb

10. 24 stripes

Chapter 2 Posttest

1. a. $\frac{4}{5}$

   b. $\frac{2}{9}$

   c. $\frac{6}{11}$

2. a. $\frac{23}{7}$

   b. $\frac{35}{8}$

   c. $\frac{167}{9}$

3. a. $5\frac{1}{3}$

   b. $16\frac{3}{4}$

   c. $20\frac{5}{7}$

4. a. $x = 36$

   b. $x = 66$

   c. $x = 13$

5. a. $1\frac{11}{60}$

   b. $8\frac{28}{45}$

   c. $\frac{53}{70}$

   d. $2\frac{21}{40}$

6. a. $\frac{8}{105}$

   b. $32\frac{13}{42}$

   c. $1\frac{1}{3}$

   d. $\frac{14}{145}$

7. $67\frac{3}{4}$ in

8. $48\frac{7}{8}$ ft

9. $1,060\frac{15}{16}$ lb

10. 61 pieces (with $6\frac{1}{4}$ in left over)

Chapter 3 Pretest

1. a. (1) $\frac{3}{8}$

   (2) $\frac{281}{500}$

   (3) $\frac{13}{50}$

   b. (1) 0.1875

   (2) 0.1379

   (3) 0.71

   c. (1) 40%

   (2) 43.33%

   (3) 18%

2. a. 0.859

   b. 8.3053

   c. 20.629

3. a. 2.51

   b. 5.326

   c. 1.423

4. a. 2.88

   b. 9.724

   c. 22.0394

5. a. 1.3

   b. 5.5

   c. 1.7459

6. a. 22.2%

   b. 86.36%

   c. 63

   d. 12.52

7. 9.97 m

8. 231.03 mL

9. 42.69 g

10. 148 sheets

Chapter 3 Posttest

1. a. (1) $\frac{7}{8}$

    (2) $\frac{171}{250}$

    (3) $\frac{19}{50}$

  b. (1) 0.5625

    (2) 0.3143

    (3) 0.56

  c. (1) 80%

    (2) 16.36%

    (3) 39%

2. a. 0.779

  b. 8.052

  c. 32.642

3. a. 3.61

  b. 3.784

  c. 13.172

4. a. 4.16

  b. 15.572

  c. 29.9345

5. a. 2.4

  b. 3.7

  c. 2.9354

6. a. 22.73%

  b. 60.71%

  c. 34.65

  d. 30.62

7. 213.2 mL

8. 0.23 cm

9. $525.35

10. 260 keys (with 0.96 cm left over)

Chapter 4 Pretest

1. a. 64
    b. 561.69
    c. 729
    d. 4.096
2. a. 13
    b. 7.88
    c. 186
    d. 5
3. a. 89.2 in
    b. 20.66 ft

4. a. 136.9 cm^2
    b. 46.9 ft^2
    c. 43.3 m^2
5. a. 2,466.73 cm^3
    b. 20.46 ft^3
    c. 2,308.39 cm^3
6. 392.5 ft
7. 1,136 ft^2
8. 4,231.6 ft^3

Chapter 4 Posttest

1. a. 196
   b. 3,769.96
   c. 1,331
   d. 12.167
2. a. 16
   b. 11.38
   c. 156.20
   d. 7
3. a. $43\frac{3}{4}$ in
   b. 42.33 in

4. a. $43\frac{11}{32}$ in^2
   b. 1349.45 cm^2
   c. 147.12 cm^2
5. a. 313.74 cm^3
   b. 411.09 in^3
   c. 43.82 in^3
6. 8 ft 5 in
7. 31.586 cm^2
8. 3,818.7 ft^3

Chapter 5 Pretest

1. a. $1\frac{3}{4}$ in
   b. 3.0 cm
   c. 27°; 64°
2. a. $6\frac{1}{4}$" to $7\frac{1}{4}$"; 1"
   b. 2.176" to 2.180"; 0.004"
   c. 4.338 mm to 4.342 mm;
      0.004 mm
3. a. 61.3 mL
   b. 7.84 g
   c. 3.517 ccf

4. a. 1.18 gal
   b. 0.3074 mi
   c. 13.5 oz
   d. 67,054 in
   e. 0.183 m
   f. 680 g
   g. 0.2185 L
   h. 0.018738 kg

Chapter 5 Posttest

1. a. $2\frac{1}{2}$ in
   b. 5.6 cm
   c. 23°; 71°
2. a. 7" to $7\frac{3}{4}$"; $\frac{3}{4}$"
   b. 1.656" to 1.662"; 0.006"
   c. 7.297 mm to 7.302 mm;
      0.005 mm
3. a. 56.7 mL
   b. 3.16 g
   c. 4,629 ccf

4. a. 9.24 qt
   b. 20.4 ft
   c. 25.24 lb
   d. 0.4358 gal
   e. 176 cm
   f. 0.8234 kg
   g. 64.5 mL
   h. 148,700 cg

Chapter 6 Pretest

1. a. $r = \frac{C}{2\pi}$

    b. $h = 2\frac{A}{b}$

2. 4.46 ft

3. 530 ft

4. 462.4 g

5. a. 2; 2 : 1

    b. $\frac{1}{3}$; 0.33 : 1

    c. $\frac{175}{42}$; 4.17 : 1

6. a. 9.33

    b. 3.5

    c. 41.66

7. 4,167 lb

8. 187.5 g

Chapter 6 Posttest

1. a. $d = \frac{p}{kh}$

    b. $s = \sqrt{\frac{A}{6}}$

2. 58 in

3. 0.0017 cm

4. 5.95 mph per second

5. a. 4; 4 : 1

    b. $\frac{3}{4}$; 0.75 : 1

    c. $\frac{7}{2}$; 3.5 : 1

6. a. 3.18

    b. 61.6

    c. 39.8

7. 15 $(14\frac{2}{7})$ gal

8. $21,579.23

Chapter 7 Pretest

1. Clerical; 132 (38%); Retail 122 (35%); Wholesale 77 (22%); Advertising 11 (3%); Maintenance 7 (2%);

2.

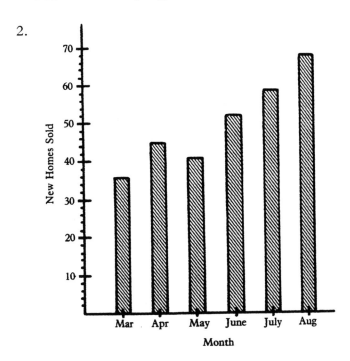

3.

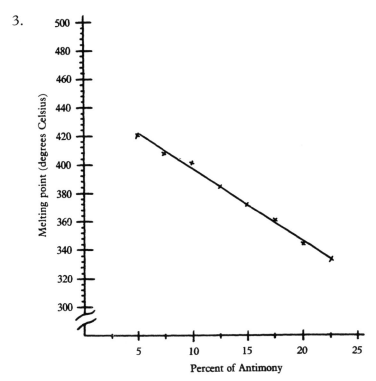

4. a. at 3:30 PM; 1,860 kwh

   b. 1,720 kwh; 1,480 kwh;

   c. Answers will vary. Straight line extrapolation gives about 1,270 kwh and about 1,180 kwh.

Chapter 7 Posttest

1.

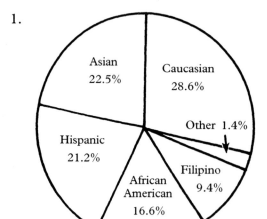

2. a. Will; 156 cars

    b. Regina; 46 cars

    c. Felix (116 cars); Will (156 cars); Sui (140 cars); Li (106 cars);
        Ann sold exactly 100 cars

3. a. 5,000; 25,000; 16,000; 30,000

    b. 1960 to 1968 and 1987 to 1993

    c. Answers will vary depending on student extrapolation. Straight line extrapolation
        gives about 44,000 and about 61,000.

4.

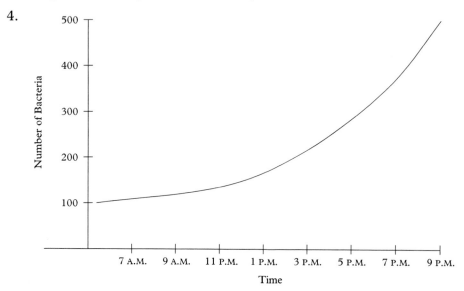

Share Your Bright Ideas with Us!

We want to hear from you! Your valuable comments and suggestions will help us meet your current and future classroom needs.

Your name_____Date_____

School name_____

School address_____

City _____State _____Zip_____Phone number (_____)_____

Grade level taught_____Subject area(s) taught_____Average class size_____

Where did you purchase this publication?_____

Was your salesperson knowledgeable about this product?   Yes_____   No_____

What monies were used to purchase this product?

____School supplemental budget   ____Federal/state funding   ____Personal

Please "grade" this Walch publication according to the following criteria:

	A	B	C	D	F
Quality of service you received when purchasing	A	B	C	D	F
Ease of use	A	B	C	D	F
Quality of content	A	B	C	D	F
Page layout	A	B	C	D	F
Organization of material	A	B	C	D	F
Suitability for grade level	A	B	C	D	F
Instructional value	A	B	C	D	F

COMMENTS:_____

_____

What specific supplemental materials would help you meet your current—or future—instructional needs?

_____

Have you used other Walch publications? If so, which ones?_____

May we use your comments in upcoming communications?   ____Yes   ____No

Please **FAX** this completed form to **207-772-3105**, or mail it to:

Product Development, J. Weston Walch, Publisher, P. O. Box 658, Portland, ME 04104-0658

We will send you a **FREE GIFT** as our way of thanking you for your feedback. **THANK YOU!**